GIANT
PRESCHOOL

This workbook belongs to

....

Dear Parents,

Welcome to the *Giant Preschool* workbook!

The fun activities in this workbook will introduce your child to key learning concepts in readiness for kindergarten. Your child will build pen-control skills, learn the conventions of print, and practice the ABCs and 123s. Here are some tips to help ensure your child gets the most from this book.

- Look at the pages with your child, ensuring he or she knows what to do before starting.

- Make the activity sessions positive experiences. Praise your child's efforts and point out when progress has been made through practice.

- Encourage your child to take as much time as is needed, rather than rushing. You can help him or her focus on the current page by pulling it out using the perforations.

- Plan for your child to do only one or two pages a day, and encourage him or her to look forward to completing another activity on another day.

- If your child makes a mistake, help foster a mindset that views mistakes as learning opportunities and suggest your child tries again.

- If possible, complete the activities within each section in order as the activities often build on one another.

- Relate the learning to things in your child's world. For example, if your child is completing a page about the color red, ask him or her to find red objects around your home.

- There are stickers to use at the back of the book. You can use them as reward stickers, or your child can use them to decorate the pages or in any way he or she likes.

We wish your child hours of enjoyment while preparing for a strong start at school!

Scholastic Early Learning

Contents

Driving Home

Trace the dotted lines to help the cars reach their garages. Start at the big red dot.

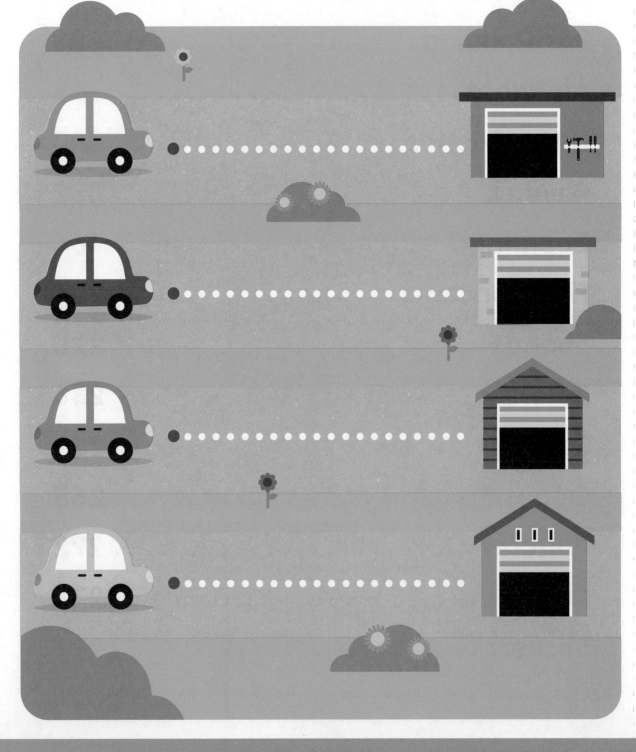

Stripes Are Cool!

Trace the stripes on the sweaters.

Lollipop Sticks

Trace the dotted lines to make sticks for the lollipops.

Build a Barn

Trace the dotted lines to make planks for the barn.

Downhill Skiing

Trace the trail down the mountain.

Zigzag Lightning

Trace the lightning bolts in the stormy sky.

Play Ball!

Trace the bouncing balls.

Big Bubbles

Trace the bubbles under the sea.

Curvy Clouds

Trace the path to help the unicorn reach the castle.

Find My Mother

Trace the paths to lead the baby animals
to their mothers.

Super Tracer

Trace the superhero.

Blast Off!

Trace the rocket.

Hiking Trail

Lead the hikers along the trail to their cabin.

start →

→ finish

Busy Burrow

Help the bunnies tunnel through the burrow.

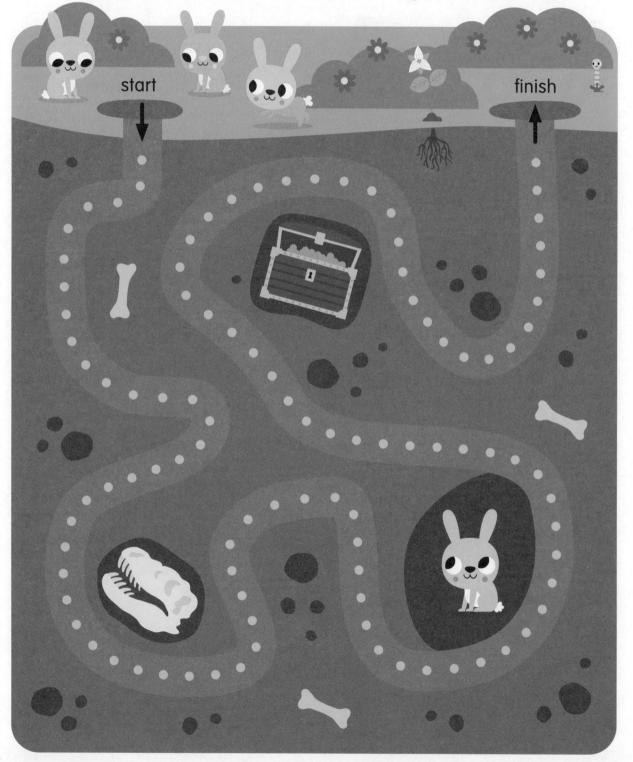

start

finish

Off to School

Trace the path to lead the bus to school.

Friendly Fish

Lead the fish to his friend without meeting any sharks.

start ➡

finish

Thirsty Dinos

Lead the lost dinosaur to the watering hole.

start →

finish

Race to the Rescue

Lead the fire truck to the fire.

start →

finish

Loopy Leaf

Help the caterpillar find its way across the leaf.

start →

finish ↓

Pumpkin Path

Help the worm wiggle its way to the center of the pumpkin.

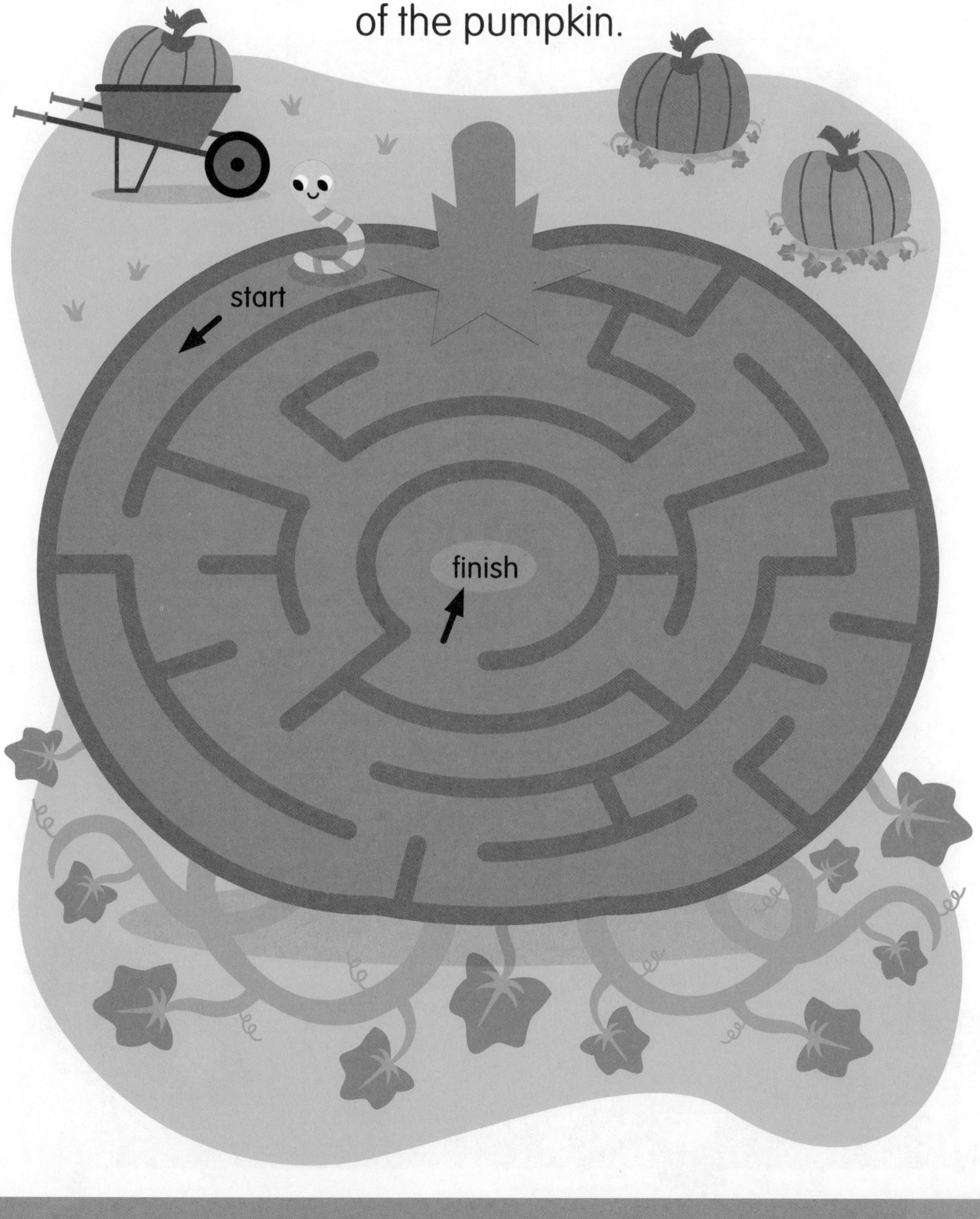

start

finish

Honeycomb Maze

Help the bee find its way out of the hive.

start

finish

Hedge Maze

Help the children find their way to the center of the hedge maze.

start

finish

Garden Grid

Draw a line linking the butterflies from start to finish.

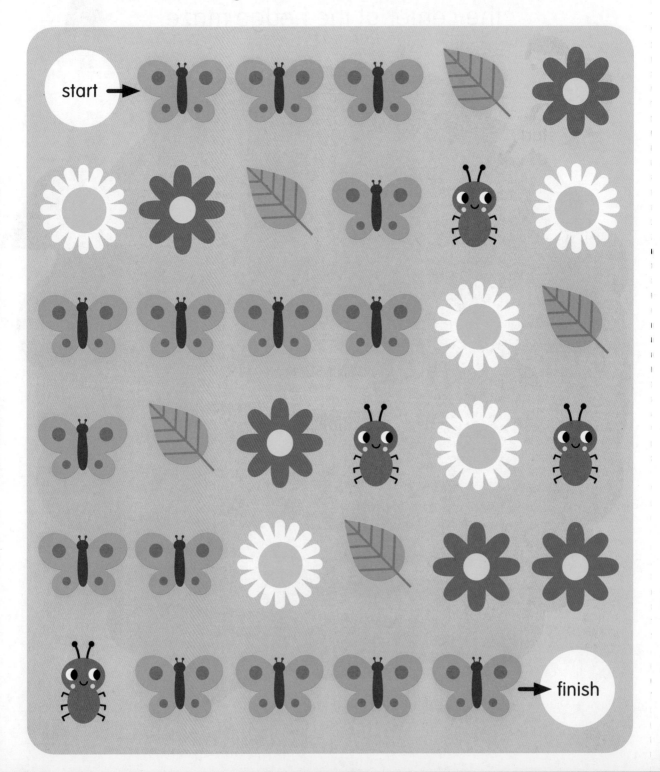

Animal Grid

Draw a line linking the cats from start to finish.

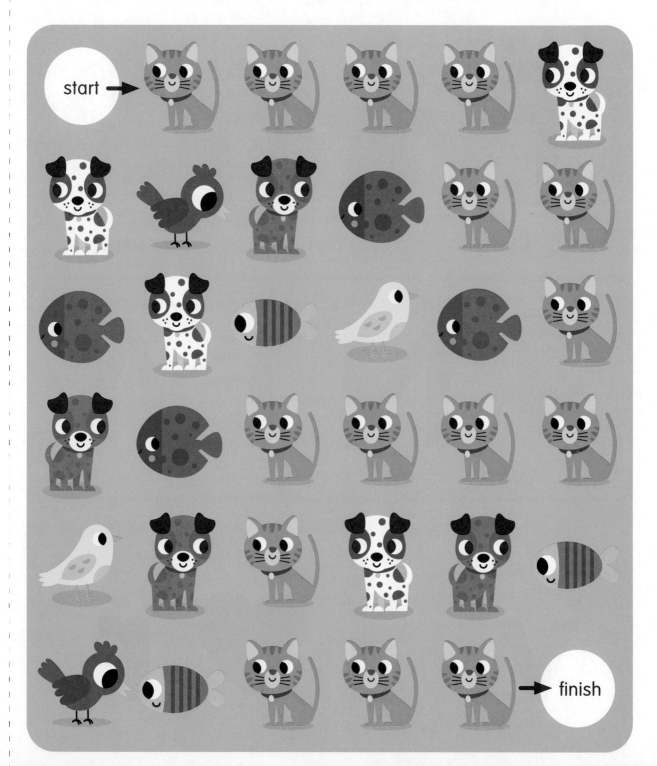

Identify Letters

Find and circle 3 letters in each line.

Find the Letters

Find and circle 8 letters in the picture.

Identify Words

A written word is made of a row of letters.
Circle 2 words in each line.

dad   go

shark   laugh

fun   pink

what   play

Find the Words

Find and circle 8 words in the picture.

Lowercase Letters

Draw lines to match the lowercase letters.

Trace the Letters

Trace the lowercase letters on the easels.

Uppercase Letters

Draw lines to match the uppercase letters.

X D O R

O A U D

R U X A

Trace the Letters

Trace the uppercase letters on the posters.

Which Direction?

In each row, circle the lowercase letter
that faces the same way as the first letter.

e	ɘ	e	ɘ
p	p	q	q
r	ɿ	r	ɿ
d	b	b	d
s	s	ƨ	ƨ

Which Direction?

In each row, circle the uppercase letter that faces the same way as the first letter.

Match the Words

Draw lines to match the words that are the same.

cow

hen

pig

barn

hen

cow

barn

duck

duck

pig

Match the Words

Draw lines to match the words that are the same.

Write Words

Use the pictures to help you read the words.
Then trace the words.

cat

hat

van

fan

king

ring

Write Words

Use the pictures to help you read the words.
Then trace the words.

car

star

goat

boat

bell

shell

Write a Sentence

A sentence is a line of words that tells us something. Look at the picture, and then trace the sentence.

I ride a bike.

Write a Sentence

Look at the picture, and then trace the sentence.

I ride a horse.

The Letter A

Finish coloring the picture. Where is the letter **a**?

Trace the uppercase and lowercase **a**'s.

Aa Aa Aa Aa

Find and Circle

Circle the words that start with **a**.

arrow   **b**us   **a**pple

crab   **a**nchor   **l**izard

The Letter B

Use the color key to reveal the letter.

Key: b = red   c = green   d = blue

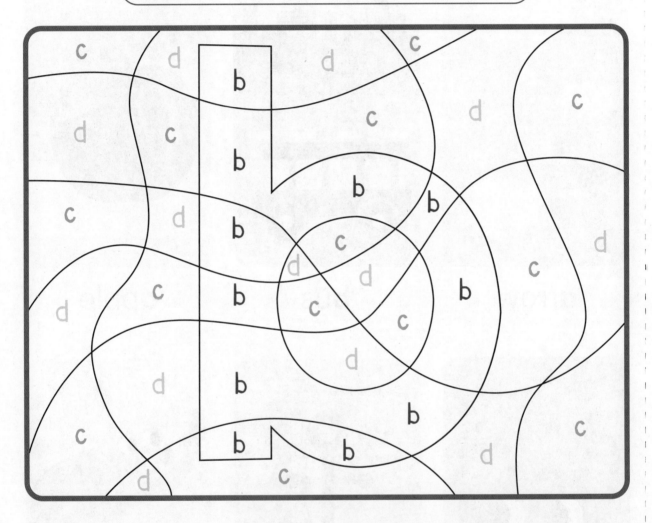

Trace the uppercase and lowercase **b**'s.

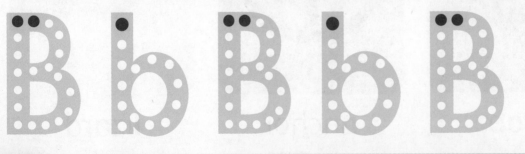

Find the B Words

Find and circle 8 things that begin with **b**.

window

box

books

car

lamp

bed

balloon

dresser

bat

rug

boy

train

ball

beanbag

The Letter C

Trace the candies to make a giant **c** on the cookie.

Trace the uppercase and lowercase **c**'s.

Find the C's

Find and circle 6 **c**'s. Then finish coloring the picture.

The Letter D

Find and circle the **d**'s in these words.

door

bed

daddy

deer

Trace the uppercase and lowercase **d**'s.

Join the Dots

Join the dots to find something that begins with **d**.
What is it?

The Letter E

Find and trace the **e**'s in these words.

beetle eye

Trace the uppercase and lowercase **e**'s.

E is for Eel

Use the color key to reveal the **ee**l.

Key: e = brown   d = blue

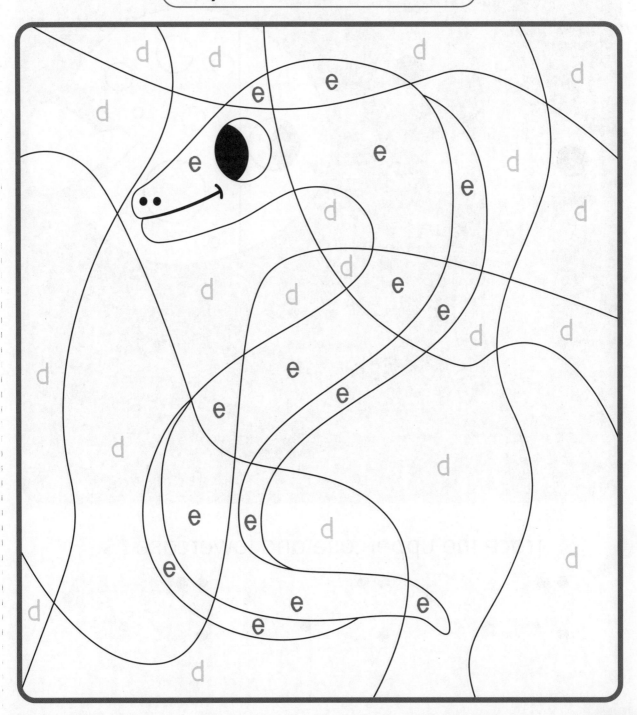

The Letter F

Trace the **f**, and then color the **f**ish your **f**avorite color.

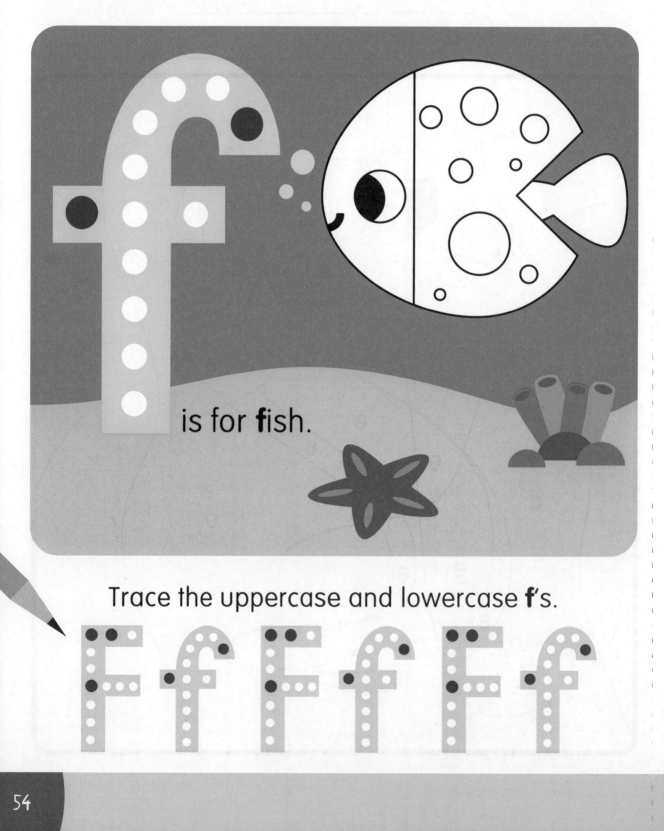

is for **f**ish.

Trace the uppercase and lowercase **f**'s.

Letter Maze

Follow the **f**'s to help **F**rank **f**ind his **f**riend.

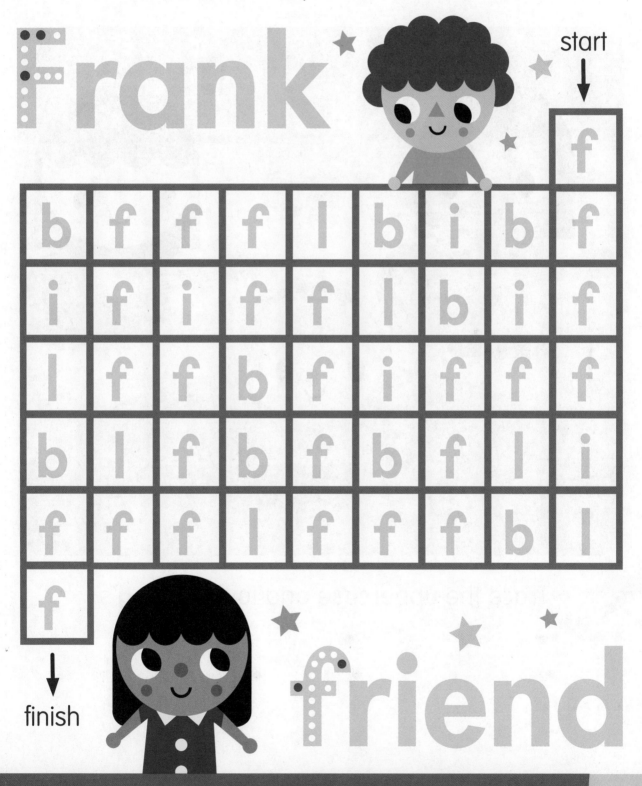

start

Frank

b f f f l b i b f

i f i f f l b i f

l f f b f i f f f

b l f b f b f l i

f f f l l f f f b l

f

finish

friend

The Letter G

Circle the **g**irl with a **g** on her **g**uitar.

Trace the uppercase and lowercase **g**'s.

G g G g G g

Find the G Words

Trace the **g**. Then draw lines from the **g**
to the things that start with **g**.

giraffe

leaf

coat

goat

glasses

elephant

The Letter H

Find and circle 5 **h**'s.

Trace the uppercase and lowercase **h**'s.

Label the Pictures

Circle the word that begins with **h**
to label each picture correctly.

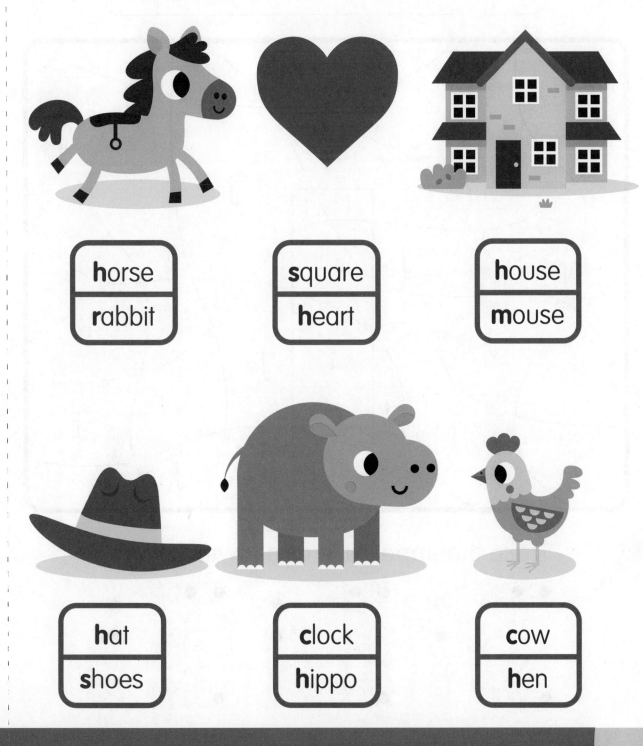

horse
rabbit

square
heart

house
mouse

hat
shoes

clock
hippo

cow
hen

The Letter I

Use the color key to reveal the letter.

Key: h = blue i = orange j = purple

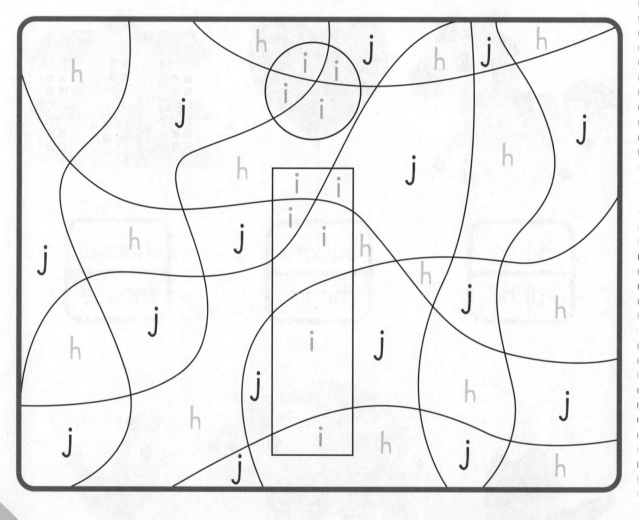

Trace the uppercase and lowercase i's.

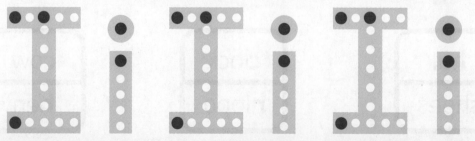

Find and Circle

Circle the words that start with **i**.

iron   **p**arrot   **i**ce

island   **s**quirrel   **b**oat

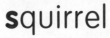

The Letter J

Finish coloring the picture. Where is the letter **j**?

Trace the uppercase and lowercase **j**'s.

Find the J Words

Find and circle 8 things that begin with **j**.

cloud

jet

Josh

tree

jack-o-lantern

Jeep

Julia

jacket

jump

grass

jeans

trampoline

The Letter K

Find and circle the **k**'s in these words.

kitten

kick

duck

kayak

Trace the uppercase and lowercase **k**'s.

Find the K's

Find and circle 6 **k**'s. Then finish coloring the picture.

The Letter L

Find and trace the **l**'s in these words.

llama lollipop

Trace the uppercase and lowercase **l**'s.

Join the Dots

Join the dots to find something that begins with **l**.
What is it?

The Letter M

Color the **m** on **M**ia's **m**ug.

Trace the uppercase and lowercase **m**'s.

MmMmMm

M is for Moon

Use the color key to reveal the **m**oon.

Key: n = blue m = yellow

The Letter N

Trace the **n**, and then color **N**ick the **n**urse.

n is for **n**urse.

Trace the uppercase and lowercase **n**'s.

Find the N Words

Trace the **n**. Then draw lines from the **n** to the things that start with **n**.

pony

nest

nose

drum

banana

net

The Letter O

Circle the **o**ctopus whose color begins with **o**.

yellow

orange

red

Trace the uppercase and lowercase **o**'s.

Label the Pictures

Circle the word that begins with **o**
to label each picture correctly.

orange
pear

bear
otter

owl
socks

onion
dress

table
orca

box
ox

The Letter P

Find and circle 5 **p**'s.

p g d p

g y p b

b d y

d g p b p

Trace the uppercase and lowercase **p**'s.

Pp Pp Pp Pp Pp

Letter Maze

Follow the **p**'s to help the **parrot** find the **peach**.

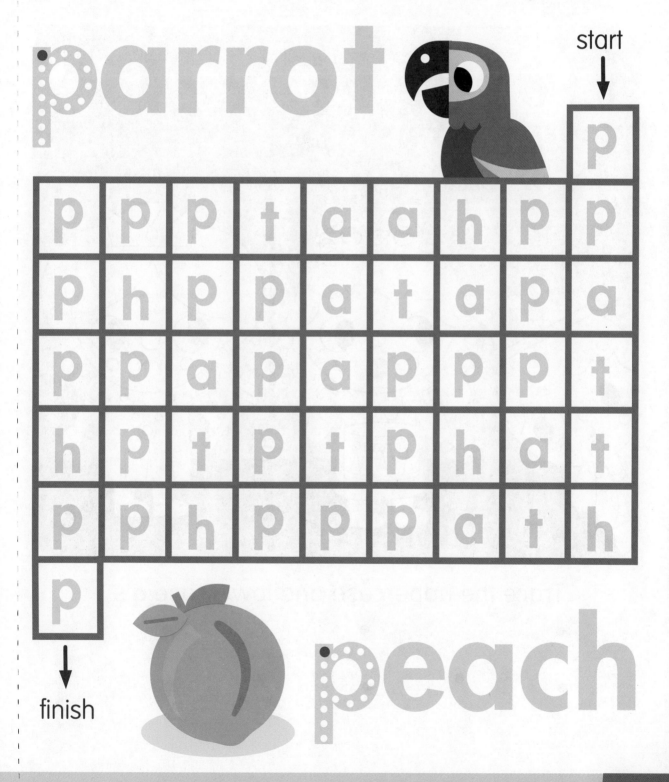

start

p

p	p	p	t	a	a	h	p	p
p	h	p	p	a	t	a	p	a
p	p	a	p	a	p	p	p	t
h	p	t	p	t	p	h	a	t
p	p	h	p	p	p	a	t	h

p

finish

peach

The Letter Q

Finish coloring the picture. Can you find the letter **q**?

Trace the uppercase and lowercase **q**'s.

Find and Circle

Circle the words that start with **q**.

penguin

quilt

dog

quack

gate

question

The Letter R

Find and circle the **r**'s in these words.

rhino

robot

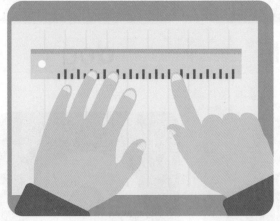

ruler

river

Trace the uppercase and lowercase **r**'s.

Find the R Words

Find and circle 8 things that begin with **r**.

tree

rainbow

bee

robin

fence

roses

rope

Ryan

rocks

swing

rabbit

rake

log

The Letter S

Find and trace the **s**'s in these words.

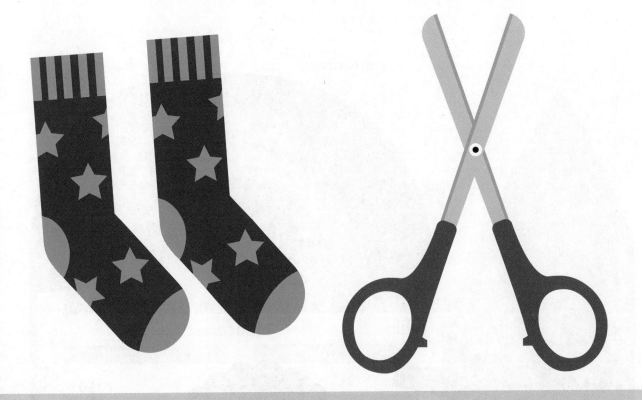

socks scissors

Trace the uppercase and lowercase **s**'s.

Find the S Words

Trace the **s**. Then draw lines from the **s** to the things that start with **s**.

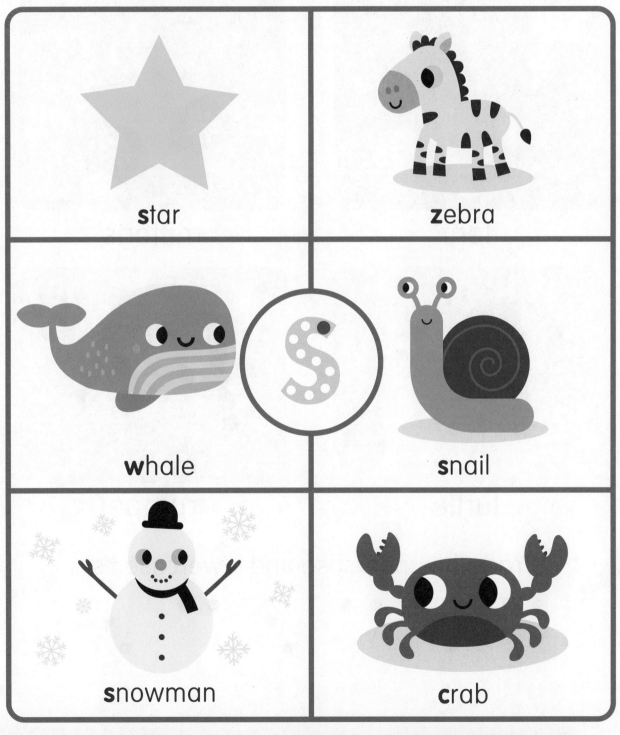

star

zebra

whale

snail

snowman

crab

The Letter T

Find and circle the **t**'s in these words.

tent

mittens

turtle

trumpet

Trace the uppercase and lowercase **t**'s.

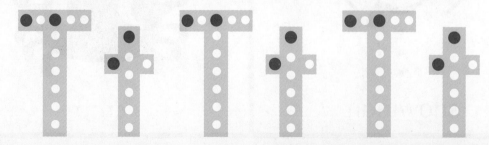

Label the Pictures

Circle the word that begins with **t**
to label each picture correctly.

house
turkey

toad
lion

teddy
book

foot
tree

tiger
mouse

chair
table

The Letter U

Use the color key to reveal the letter.

Key: u = green v = pink w = red

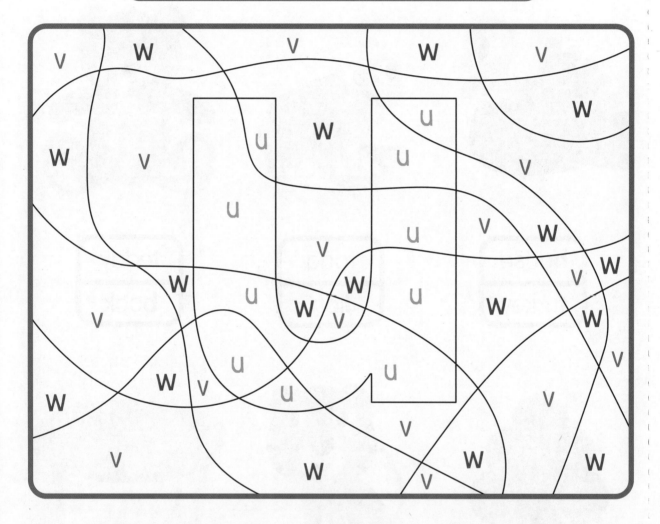

Trace the uppercase and lowercase **u**'s.

Letter Maze

Follow the **u**'s to help **U**na find her **u**k**u**lele.

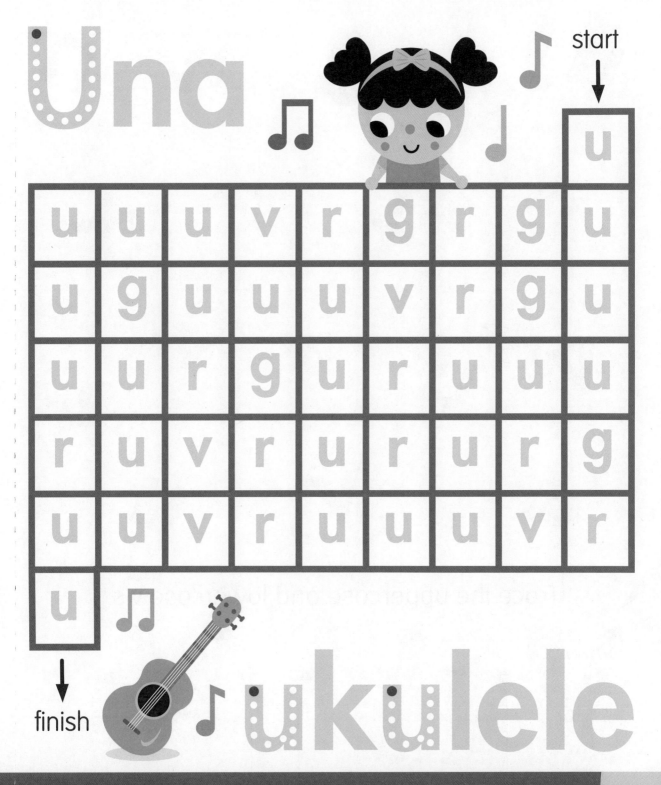

The Letter V

Find and circle 5 **v**'s.

u v u w n

v

n x v x

v u n w

v

x v u

Trace the uppercase and lowercase **v**'s.

VvVvVvVvVv

V is for Van

Use the color key to reveal the **v**an.

Key: v = red w = green

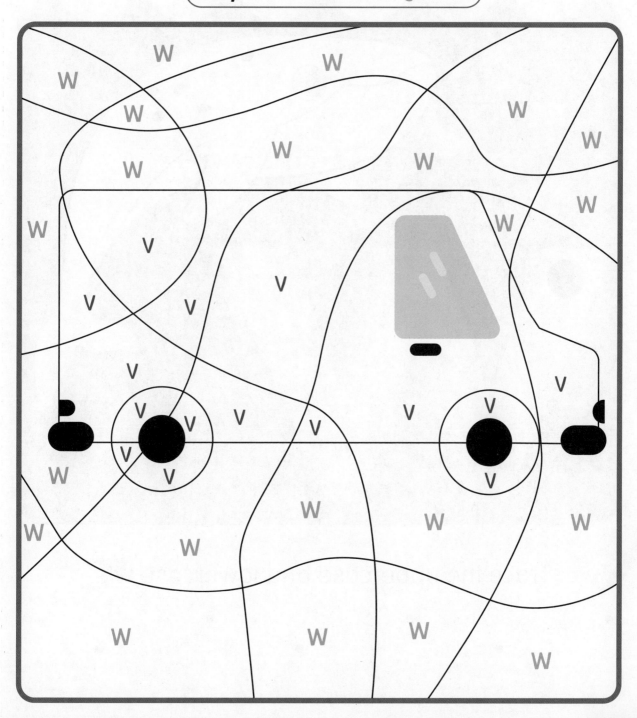

The Letter W

Trace the **w**. Then color the **w**hale in the **w**avy **w**ater.

is for **w**hale.

Trace the uppercase and lowercase **w**'s.

Find the W's

Find and circle 6 **w**'s. Then finish coloring the picture.

The Letter X

Trace the **x** on the treasure map.
Then finish coloring the map.

Trace the uppercase and lowercase **x**'s.

Find the X's

Find and circle 6 **x**'s. Then finish coloring the picture.

The Letter Y

Find and circle the **y**'s in these words.

yellow

yummy

yo-yo

baby

Trace the uppercase and lowercase **y**'s.

Join the Dots

Join the dots to reveal the **y**acht.

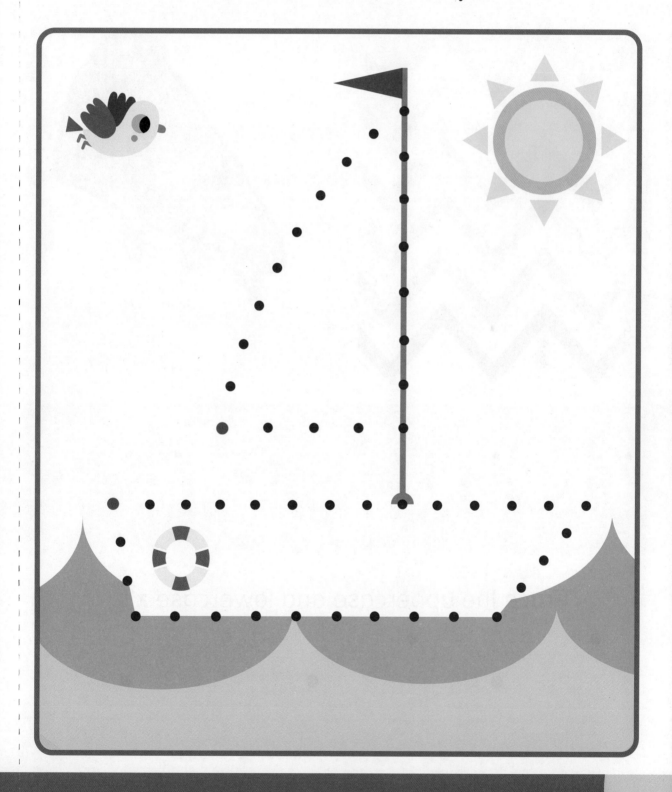

The Letter Z

Find and trace the **z**'s in these words.

zigzags pizza

Trace the uppercase and lowercase **z**'s.

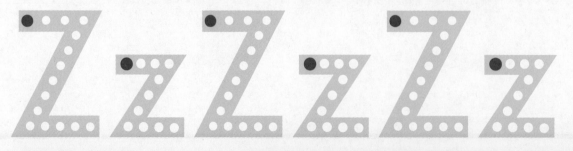

Find and Circle

Circle the words that start with **z**.

 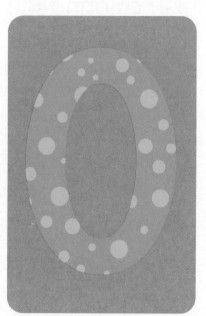 

monkey   **z**ero   **s**nail

wolf   **z**oo   **z**ebra

Alphabet Dots

Join the lowercase letters in alphabetical order.
Then finish coloring the page.

Lowercase Maze

Help the baby turtle reach the ocean by following the letters in alphabetical order.

start

finish

Alphabet Dots

Join the uppercase letters in alphabetical order. Then finish coloring the page.

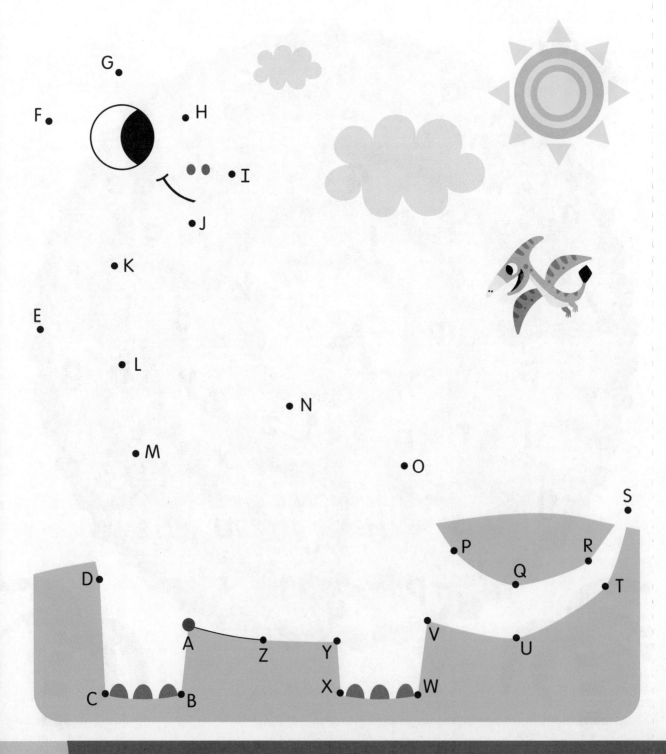

Uppercase Maze

Help the plane reach the airport by following the letters in alphabetical order.

The S Sound

Listen for the **s sound** as you say each word.
Then trace the **s**'s and the **c**'s.

seal   sisters

city   cereal

Find the S Words

Color the **s**-shaped snake. Then circle other things that begin with the **s** sound.

The Short A Sound

Listen for the **a sound** as you say each word.
Then trace the **a**'s.

hat   bag

van   dad

Listen for A

Draw a line from the animals that have
a **short a sound** in the middle to the giant **a**.

ram

dog

hen

bat

rat

pig

cat

The T Sound

Listen for the **t sound** as you say each word.
Then trace the **t**'s.

toad table

tent tomato

T in a Sentence

Trace the **t**'s. Then finish coloring the picture.

Tim saw two tiny

tigers in tutus.

The M Sound

Listen for the **m sound** as you say each word.
Then trace the **m**'s.

mouse mouth

mermaid milk

Find the M Words

Color the **m**-shaped monster. Then circle other things that begin with the **m sound**.

The P Sound

Listen for the **p sound** as you say each word.
Then trace the **p**'s.

pond pencil

paint parrot

Count the P's

Count the **p**'s in each word.
Then draw a line from the word to the number.

po**pp**y

pu**pp**y

1 2 3

pu**pp**et

pum**p**kin

pear

The Short I Sound

Listen for the **i sound** as you say each word.
Then trace the **i**'s.

six   hill

skip   fish

Listen for I

Circle the word in each pair that has
the **i sound** in the middle.

bib
bob

dig
dog

pug
pig

lid
lad

list
lost

trap
trip

ship
shop

swam
swim

The N Sound

Listen for the **n sound** as you say each word.
Then trace the **n**'s.

nest   nurse

nose   nine

Start or End?

Use a **green** pencil to circle the words
that **start** with an **n sound**.
Use a **red** pencil to circle the words
that **end** with an **n sound**.

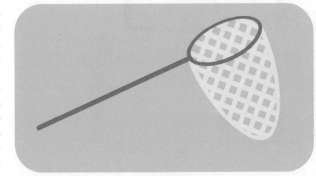

net

lion

rain

night

ten

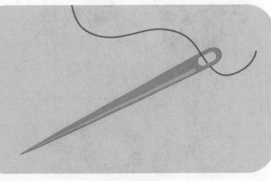

needle

The D Sound

Listen for the **d sound** as you say each word.
Then trace the **d**'s.

duck

desk

dice

dove

D in a Sentence

Trace the **d**'s. Then finish coloring the picture.

Dad's dog Dexter

dives down deep.

The K Sound

Listen for the **k sound** as you say each word.
Then trace the **k**'s and **c**'s.

key

king

cap

corn

The Hard C

Circle the **c words** that have the **k sound** (hard c).
Put an "x" over the **c words** that have the **s sound** (soft c).

cat

celery

coat

cymbals

cow

cup

The Short O Sound

Listen for the **o sound** as you say each word.
Then trace the **o**'s.

fox   hop

sock   frog

Listen for O

Circle the word in each pair that has the **o sound** in the middle.

tap
top

pop
pup

mop
map

sick
sock

math
moth

dog
dig

lock
luck

knot
knit

The G Sound

Listen for the **g sound** as you say each word.
Then trace the **g**'s.

girl   goal

golf   goose

Start or End?

Use a **blue** pencil to circle the words
that **start** with a **g sound**.
Use an **orange** pencil to circle the words
that **end** with a **g sound**.

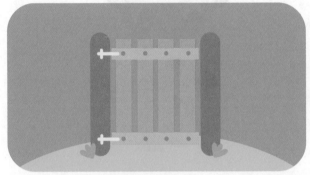

gate

egg

dog

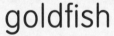
goldfish

pig

goat

The Short E Sound

Listen for the **e sound** as you say each word.
Then trace the **e**'s.

bed   vet

bell   steps

Listen for E

Circle the word in each pair that has the **e sound** in the middle.

man
men

red
rid

not
net

leg
log

jet
jut

tint
tent

bench
bunch

dress
dross

The R Sound

Listen for the **r sound** as you say each word.
Then trace the **r**'s.

rose   rake

rope   ring

R in a Sentence

Trace the **r**'s. Then finish coloring the picture.

Ruby Rabbit rode in a red rocket.

The Short U Sound

Listen for the **u sound** as you say each word.
Then trace the **u**'s.

jump hug

pup drum

Listen for U

Draw a line from the vehicles that have a **u sound** in the middle to the giant **u**.

truck

taxi

plane

sub

tug

bike

bus

The B Sound

Listen for the **b sound** as you say each word.
Then trace the **b**'s.

bear   boy

boat bird

Count the B's

Count the **b**'s in each word.
Then draw a line from the word to the number.

ba**b**y

bug

1 2 3

bum**b**le**b**ee

bu**bb**les

ba**b**oon

129

The H Sound

Listen for the **h sound** as you say each word.
Then trace the **h**'s.

hare   hose

hive   hand

Listen for H

Circle the words that start with the **h sound**. Put an "x" over the words that don't start with the **h sound**.

home

horn

barn

hammer

hook

cheese

The F Sound

Listen for the **f sound** as you say each word.
Then trace the **f**'s.

fork   fish

fox   feet

F in a Sentence

Trace the **f**'s. Then finish coloring the picture.

Meet five friends from Finn's farm.

The L Sound

Listen for the **l sound** as you say each word.
Then trace the **l**'s.

leaf lamp

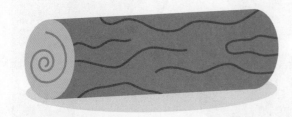

log lemon

Listen for L

Draw a line from the **l** words to the giant **l**.

leopard

lunchbox

star

mouse

unicorn

lips

lamb

The V Sound

Listen for the **v sound** as you say each word.
Then trace the **v**'s.

vase  violin

vest volcano
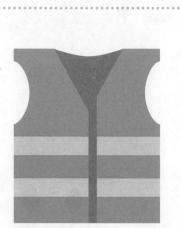

V is for Valentine

Trace the **v**'s on the Valentine's Day cards.
Then finish coloring the page.

To Vicky

To Victor

To Violet

To Vinny

The J Sound

Listen for the **j sound** as you say each word.
Then trace the **j**'s and **g**'s.

jeans giant

jog giraffe

Listen for J

Trace the **j**'s. Then finish coloring the picture.

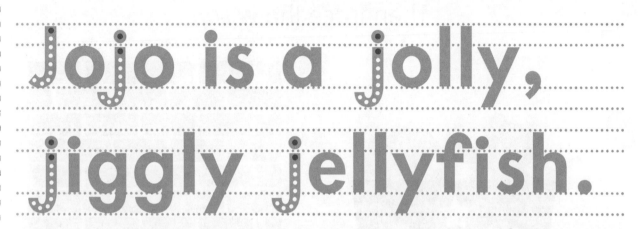

Jojo is a jolly, jiggly jellyfish.

The W Sound

Listen for the **w sound** as you say each word.
Then trace the **w**'s.

wagon wall

web wolf

Listen for W

Circle the words that start with the **w sound**.
Put an "x" over the words that don't start with the **w sound**.

watch

train

worm

wink

chair

wand

The Y Sound

Listen for the **y sound** as you say each word.
Then trace the **y**'s.

yoga   yolk

yes   yak

Follow the Trail

Follow the **y**ellow **y**arn to find
Yasmin's **y**ellow sweater.

The X Sound

Listen for the **x sound** as you say each word.
Then trace the **x**'s.

box

six

tux

ox

Listen for X

Circle the words that end with the **x sound**. Put an "x" over the words that don't end with the **x sound**.

wax

boot

mix

fix

fork

sax

The Z Sound

Listen for the **z sound** as you say each word.
Then trace the **z**'s.

zero zebra

zoom zoo

Listen for Z

Buzz like a bee. Can you hear the **z sound**?
Now trace the **z**'s.

buzz

buzz

buzz

The Ch Sound

Circle the words that start with the **ch sound**. Put an "x" over the words that don't start with the **ch sound**.

cheese

cat

chick

child

fire

cherries

Listen for Sh

Circle the word that starts with the **sh sound**.

shoe   moo

hurt   shirt

shop   hop

sorts   shorts

sell   shell

said   shed

sheep   heap

shark   bark

The Th Sound

Use a **pink** pencil to circle the words
that **start** with a **th sound**.
Use a **blue** pencil to circle the words
that **end** with a **th sound**.

thumb

path

bath

three

throw

moth

The Wh Sound

Listen for the **wh sound** as you say each word.
Then trace the **wh**'s.

whale whistle

wheel whisper

The -an Rhyme

Trace **-an** in these words.

fan

man

can

pan

Find and circle **-an** in this sentence.

Jan ran faster than Nan.

The -at Rhyme

Trace **-at** in these words.

cat

bat

mat

hat

Find and circle **-at** in this sentence.

I pat that fat cat.

The -ed Rhyme

Trace **-ed** in these words.

bed

red

shed

fed

Find and circle **-ed** in this sentence.

Fred has a red bed.

The -en Rhyme

Trace **-en** in these words.

men

hen

pen

ten

Find and circle **-en** in this sentence.

Jen has ten red hens.

The -ig Rhyme

Trace **-ig** in these words.

pig

wig

fig

dig

Find and circle **-ig** in this sentence.

A big pig did a jig.

The -in Rhyme

Trace **-in** in these words.

pin

win

fin

bin

Find and circle **-in** in this sentence.

Erin grins at her twin.

The -og Rhyme

Trace **-og** in these words.

log

jog

dog

frog

Find and circle **-og** in this sentence.

A frog jogs on a log.

The -op Rhyme

Trace **-op** in these words.

hop

pop

top

chop

Find and circle **-op** in this sentence.

I hop and bop till I drop.

The -ug Rhyme

Trace **-ug** in these words.

bug

hug

mug

rug

Find and circle **-ug** in this sentence.

A bug tugs on a rug.

The -un Rhyme

Trace **-un** in these words.

sun

bun

run

fun

Find and circle **-un** in this sentence.

The fun run has begun.

Animal Rhymes

Say the animal names aloud. Then draw lines to match each animal with its rhyming partner.

cat

moose

moth

dog

frog

bat

goose

sloth

Find the Rhyme

In each row, circle the word that rhymes with the first word.

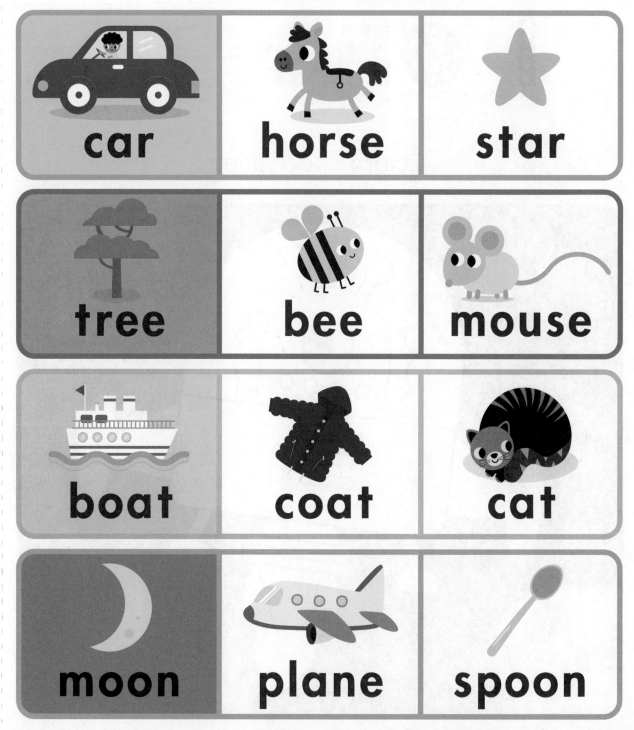

car	horse	star
tree	bee	mouse
boat	coat	cat
moon	plane	spoon

The Number 1

Trace the number and the word.

Color **1** spaceship.

Find One

Circle the walker with **1** dog.

The Number 2

Trace the number and the word.

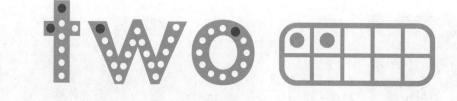

Color **2** tractors.

Trace 2

Trace **2** ice-cream sundaes.

The Number 3

Trace the number and the word.

3 three

Color **3** hooting owls.

Find Three

Circle the school with **3** fish in it.

The Number 4

Trace the number and the word.

4 four

Color **4** tigers.

Trace 4

Trace **4** party hats.

The Number 5

Trace the number and the word.

Color **5** high-flying planes.

Find Five

Circle the tower that is **5** stories high.

The Number 6

Trace the number and the word.

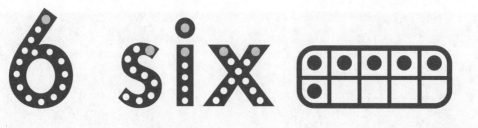

Color **6** seashells.

Trace 6

Trace **6** yellow ducklings.

The Number 7

Trace the number and the word.

7 seven

Color **7** crawling crabs.

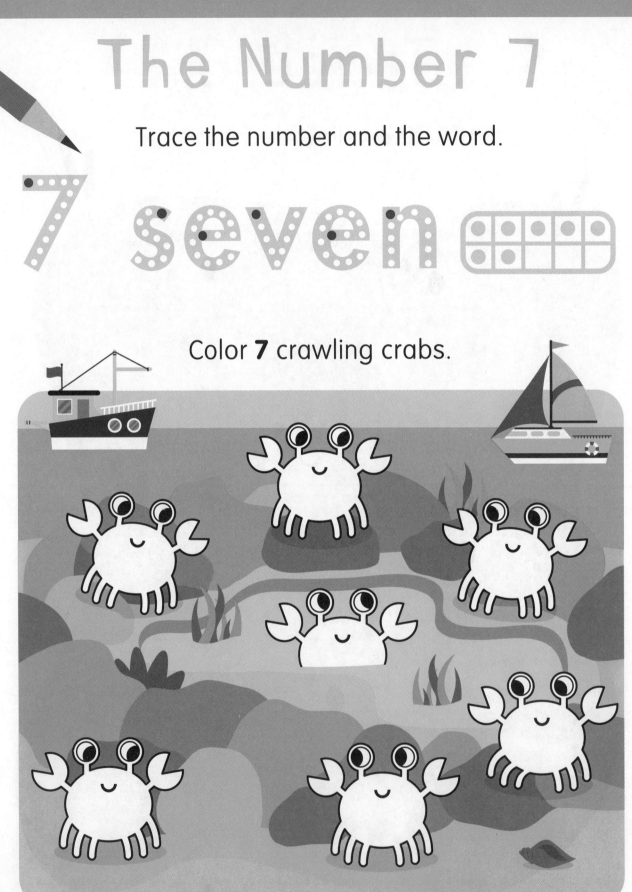

Find Seven

Circle the ladybug with **7** spots.

The Number 8

Trace the number and the word.

8 eight

Finish coloring **8** pieces of fruit.

Trace 8

Trace **8** fresh donuts.

The Number 9

Trace the number and the word.

9 nine

Color **9** cool cars.

Find Nine

Circle the train with **9** children.

The Number 10

Trace the number and the word.

Color **10** jiggly jellyfish.

Trace 10

Trace **10** birthday balloons.

The Number 11

Trace the number and the word.

11 eleven

Count **10** buttons, and color **1** more to make **11**.

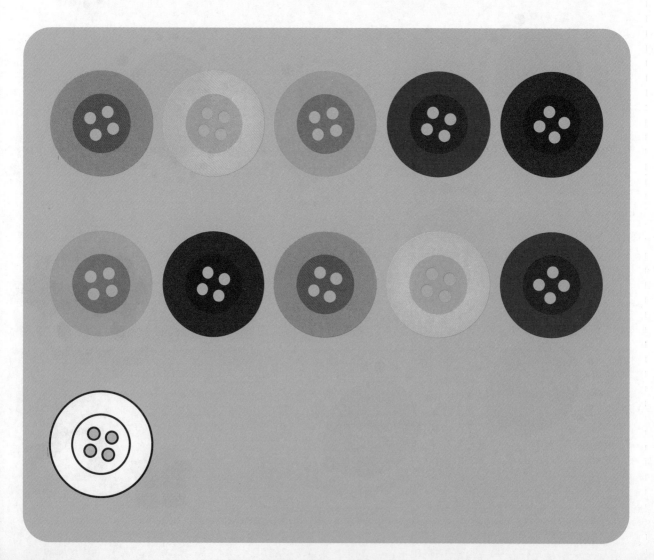

11 Bunny Hops

Trace and count **11** bunny hops to get the rabbit to the radishes.

1
2
3
4
5
6
7
8
9
10
11

The Number 12

Trace the number and the word.

12 twelve

Count **10** apples, and color **2** more to make **12**.

12 Garden Snails

Find and circle **12** snails in the garden.
Cross out the numbers as you find them.

The Number 13

Trace the number and the word.

13 thirteen

Count **10** hearts, and color **3** more to make **13**.

13 Woodland Signs

Follow the signs from **1** to **13** to lead the children through the woods.

The Number 14

Trace the number and the word.

14 fourteen

Count **10** tulips, and color **4** more to make **14**.

14 Busy Aliens

Find and circle **14** aliens on the purple planet.
Cross out the numbers as you find them.

1 2 3 4 5 6 7 8
9 10 11 12 13 14

The Number 15

Trace the number and the word.

15 fifteen

Count **10** arrows, and color **5** more to make **15**.

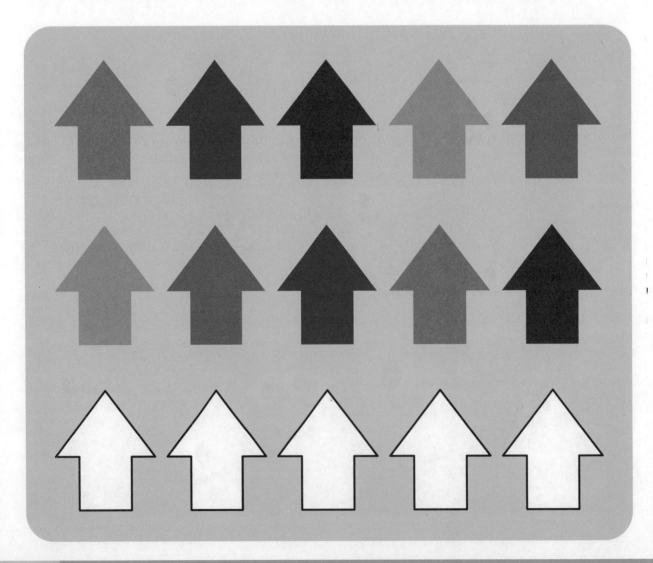

15 Dino Footprints

Follow the footprints from **1** to **15** to find the dinosaur.

The Number 16

Trace the number and the word.

16 sixteen

Count **10** trees, and color **6** more to make **16**.

16 Monkeys

Find and circle **16** monkeys in the jungle scene.
Cross out the numbers as you find them.

1 2 3 4 5 6 7 8 9
10 11 12 13 14 15 16

The Number 17

Trace the number and the word.

17 seventeen

Count **10** basketballs, and color **7** more to make **17**.

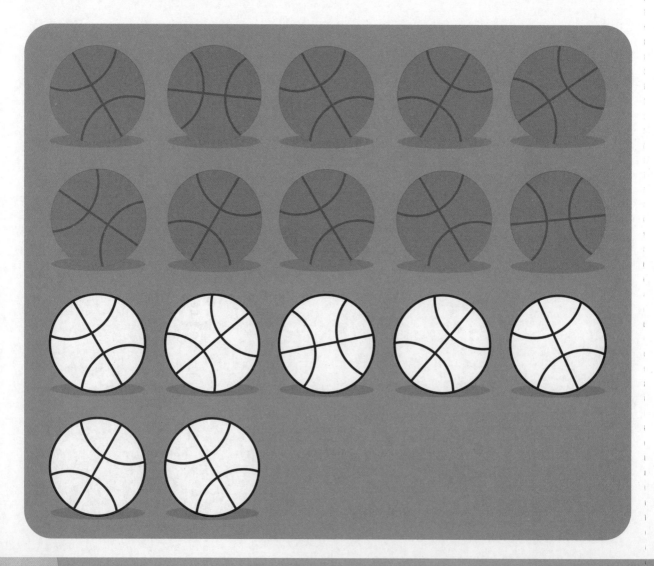

Join 17 Dots

Join the numbers from 1 to 17 to reveal the picture.

The Number 18

Trace the number and the word.

18 eighteen

Count **10** boots, and color **8** more to make **18**.

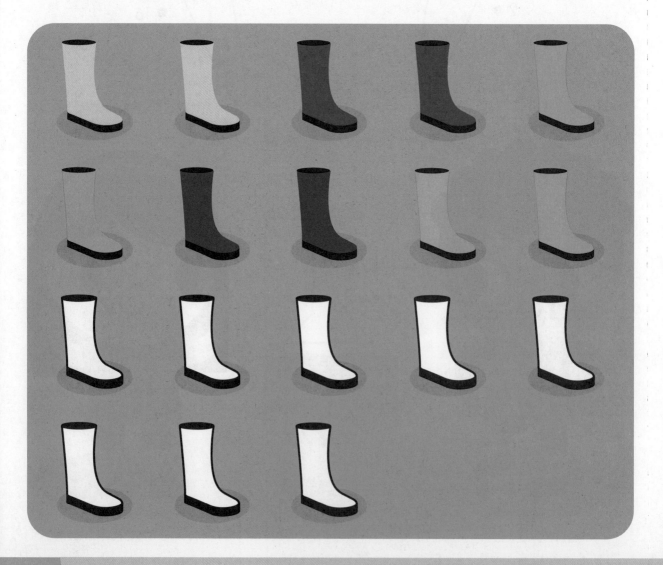

18 Happy Children

Find and circle **18** children in the playground.
Cross out the numbers as you find them.

1 2 3 4 5 6 7 8 9 10 11
12 13 14 15 16 17 18

The Number 19

Trace the number and the word.

19 nineteen

Count **10** smiley faces, and color **9** more to make **19**.

Join 19 Dots

Join the numbers from **1** to **19** to reveal the picture.

The Number 20

Trace the number and the word.

20 twenty

Count **10** stars, and color **10** more to make **20**.

20 Chirping Chicks

Find and circle **20** chicks in the farmyard.
Cross out the numbers as you find them.

1 2 3 4 5 6 7 8 9 10 11 12
13 14 15 16 17 18 19 20

Tall and Short

Circle the **tallest** building. Then draw a **taller** one.

Circle the **shortest** flower. Then draw a **shorter** one.

Long and Short

Circle the **longest** one in each row.

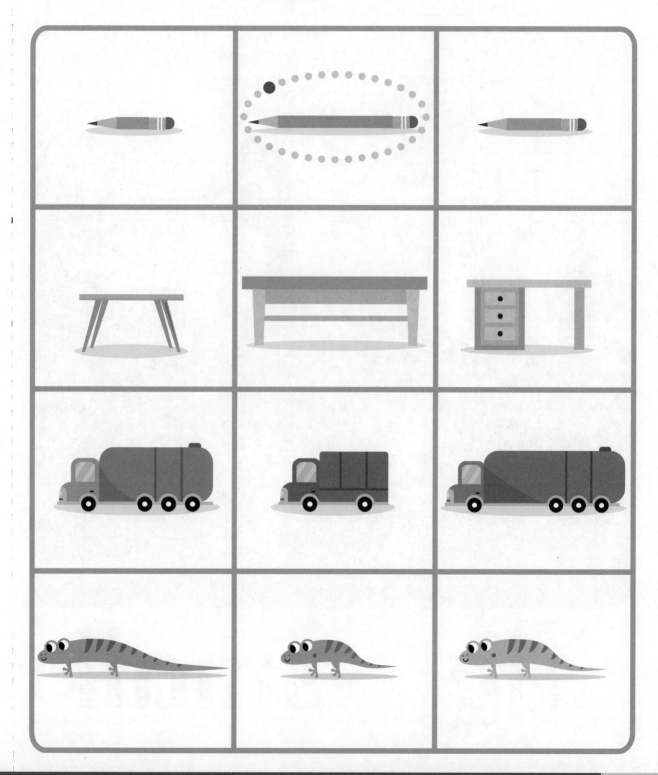

Big and Small

Circle the **biggest** dinosaur. Then trace the words.

big   small

Wide and Narrow

Draw a line from the **narrow** car to the **narrow** garage.
Draw a line from the **wide** car to the **wide** garage.

narrow

wide

High and Low

Circle the boy who is up high with a **green** pencil.
Circle the boy who is down low with a **purple** pencil.

Over and Under

Color the birds that are **under** the tree **red**.
Color the birds that are **over** the tree **blue**.

In Front or Behind

Circle the cows that are **behind** the gate.
Cross out the cow that is **in front** of the gate.

Near or Far

Circle the dragon that is **near** the fire.
Cross out the dragon that is **far** from the fire.

First and Last

Circle the dog that will reach the bowl **first**.
Then trace the words.

last   first

Above and Below

Draw the sun **above** the rowboat.
Draw some more fish **below** the rowboat.

above

below

Up and Down

Color the bear that is going **up** the hill **blue**.
Color the bear that is going **down** the hill **pink**.

up

down

Top and Bottom

Circle the one that is on the **top** of each stack.

Circle the one that is on the **bottom** of each stack.

More or Less

Circle the one that has **more** in each row.

Circle the one that has **less** in each row.

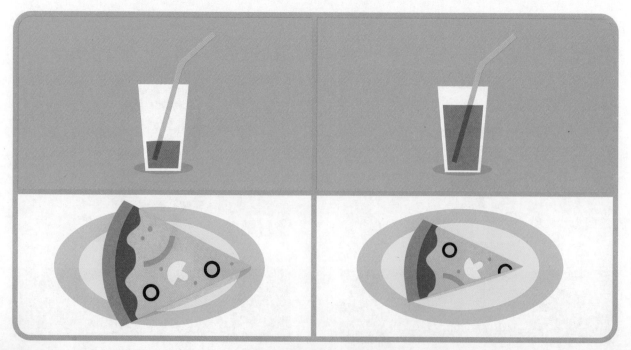

More or Fewer

Which twin has **more** cars? Color her cars **green**.
Which twin has **fewer** cars? Color her cars **red**.

In and Out

Color the cat that is **in** the box **orange**.
Color the cat that is **out** of the box **brown**.

Inside and Outside

Draw a person **outside** the house. Draw another person **inside** the house looking out the window.

inside

outside

Circles

Trace the circle in the middle. Then draw lines from the circle to the things that are circle shaped.

Circle Art

Finish coloring the circles. Use any colors you like.

Triangles

Trace the triangle in the middle. Then draw lines from the triangle to the things that are triangle shaped.

Triangle Art

Finish coloring the triangles. Use any colors you like.

Squares

Trace the square in the middle. Then draw lines from the square to the things that are square shaped.

Square Art

Finish coloring the squares. Use any colors you like.

Rectangles

Trace the rectangle in the middle. Then draw lines from the rectangle to the things that are rectangle shaped.

Rectangle Art

Finish coloring the rectangles. Use any colors you like.

Hearts

Trace the heart in the middle. Then draw lines from the heart to the things that are heart shaped.

Heart Art

Finish coloring the hearts. Use any colors you like.

Diamonds

Trace the diamond in the middle. Then draw lines from the diamond to the things that are diamond shaped.

Diamond Art

Finish coloring the diamonds. Use any colors you like.

Ovals

Trace the oval in the middle. Then draw lines from the oval to the things that are oval shaped.

Oval Art

Finish coloring the ovals. Use any colors you like.

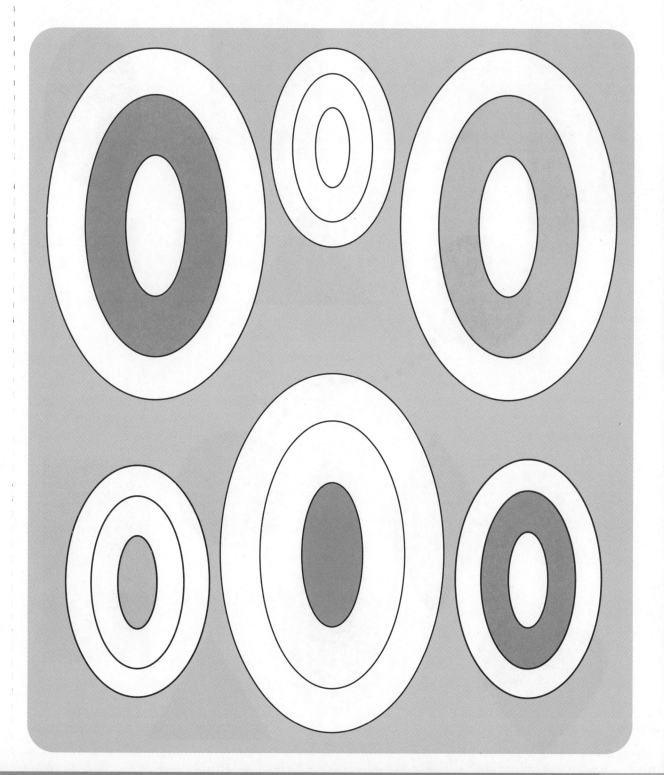

Match the Shapes

Draw lines to match the shapes that are the same.

Match the Shapes

Draw lines to match the objects of the same shape.

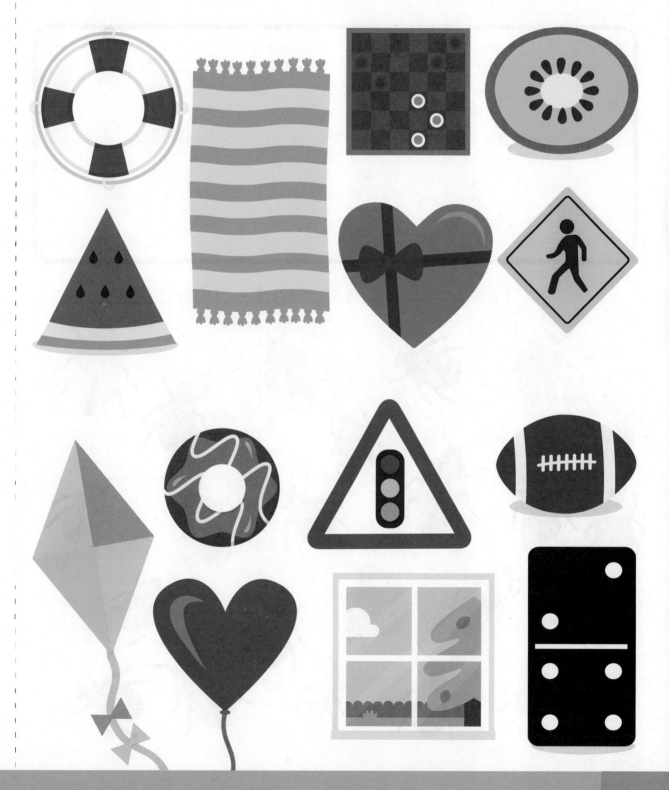

Make It Red

Color the word **red** with a **red** pencil or crayon.

Red

Find and circle the **red** beetles.

A Red Bird

Color the bird **red**.

Make It Green

Color the word **green** with a **green** pencil or crayon.

Find and circle the **green** pencils and crayons.

Which Are Green?

Put a check by the things that are **green**.
Put an "x" by the things that are not **green**.

Make It Blue

Color the word **blue** with a **blue** pencil or crayon.

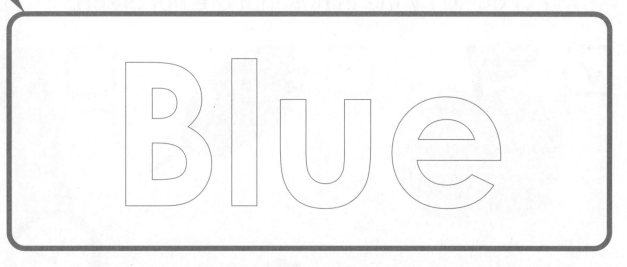

Find and circle the **blue** building blocks.

A Blue Whale

Color the whale **blue**.

Make It Orange

Color the word **orange** with an **orange** pencil or crayon.

Orange

Find and circle the **orange** balls.

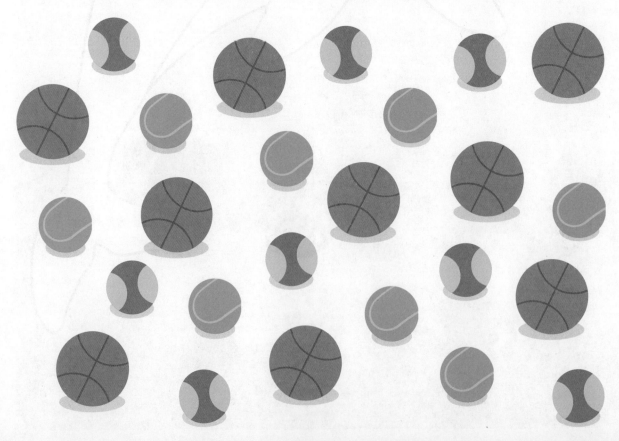

Which Are Orange?

Put a check by the things that are orange.
Put an "x" by the things that are not orange.

Make It Purple

Color the word **purple** with a **purple** pencil or crayon.

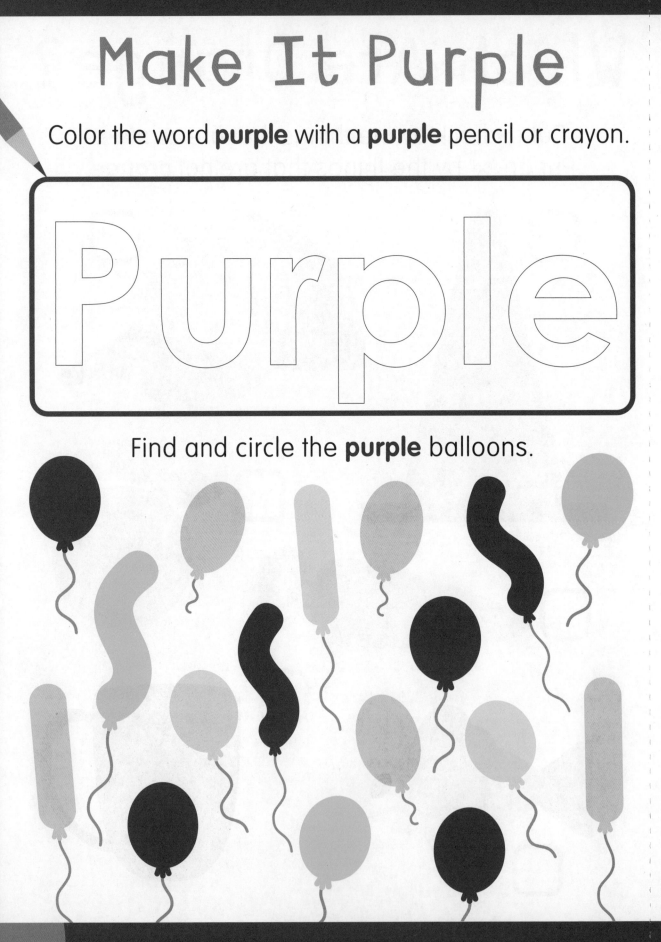

Purple

Find and circle the **purple** balloons.

A Purple Dress

Color the girl's dress **purple**.

Make It Yellow

Color the word **yellow** with
a **yellow** pencil or crayon.

Yellow

Find and circle the **yellow** flowers.

Which Are Yellow?

Put a check by the things that are yellow.
Put an "x" by the things that are not yellow.

Make It Pink

Color the word **pink** with a **pink** pencil or crayon.

Pink

Find and circle the **pink** Popsicles.

A Pink Flamingo

Color the flamingo **pink**.

Make It Brown

Color the word **brown** with a **brown** pencil or crayon.

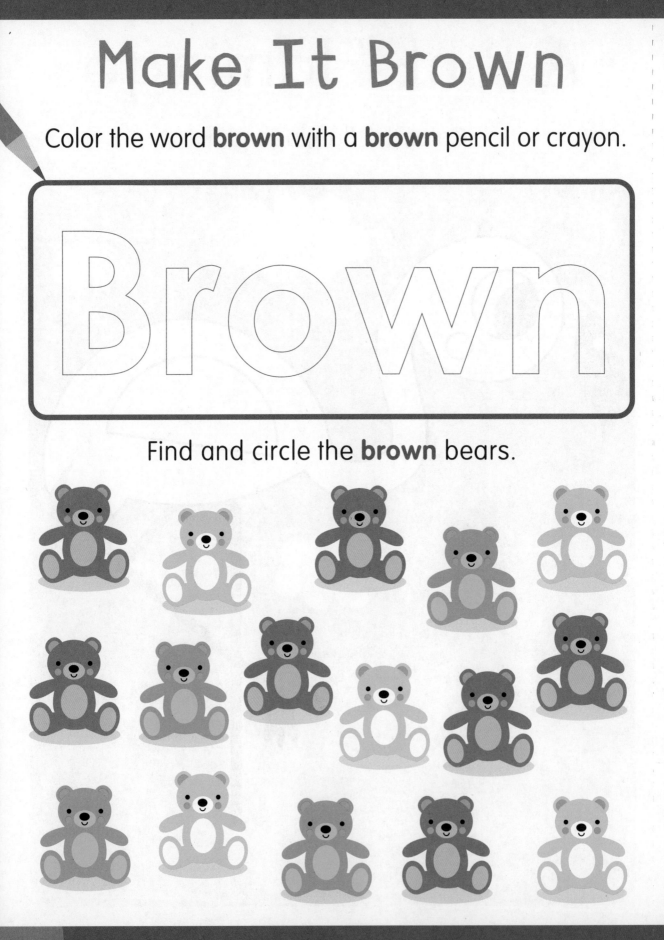

Brown

Find and circle the **brown** bears.

Which Are Brown?

Put a check by the things that are **brown**.
Put an "x" by the things that are not **brown**.

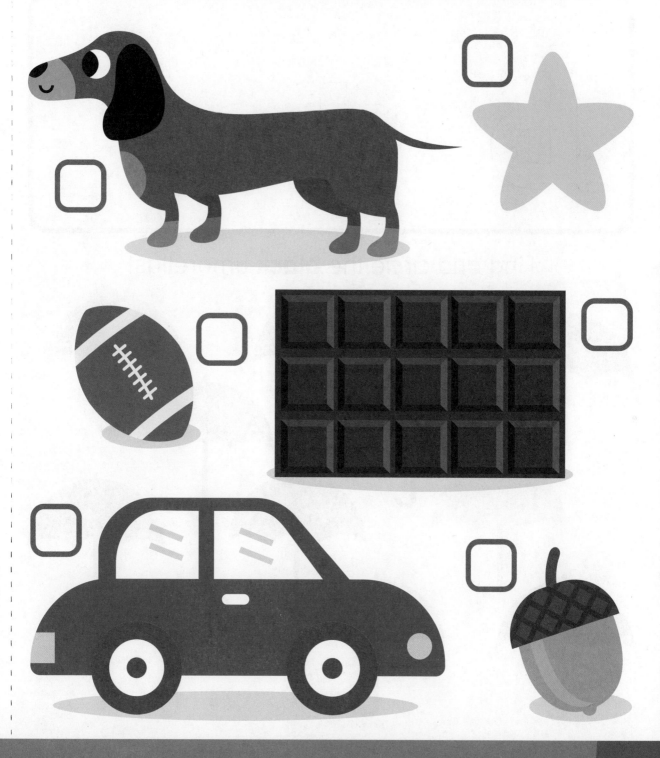

Make It Black

Color the word **black** with a **black** pencil or crayon.

Find and circle the **black** umbrellas.

A Black Bat

Color the bat **black**.

Match Vehicles

Draw lines to match the vehicles that are the same.

Match Dinosaurs

Draw lines to match the dinosaurs that are the same.

Match Twins

Draw lines to match the identical twins.

Match Clothes

Draw lines to match the clothes of the same type.

Same and Different

In each row, circle the picture that is different from the first one.

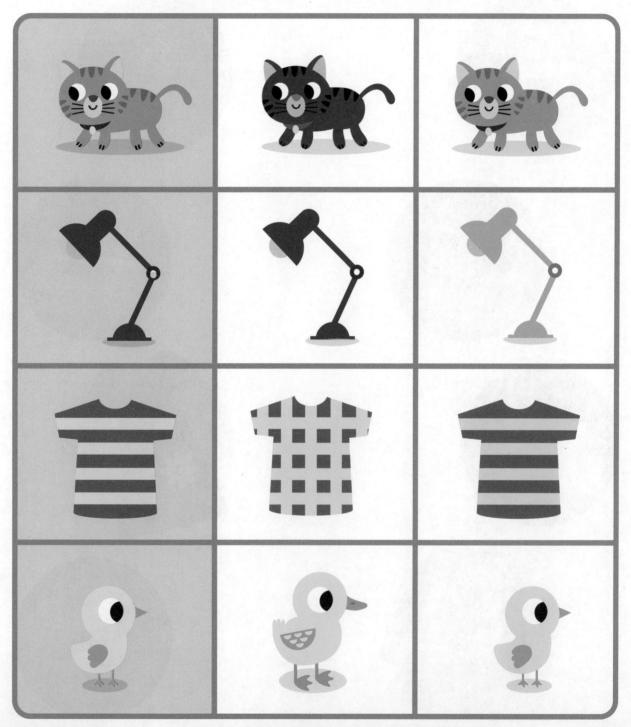

Find the Match

Find and circle these things in the picture.

Same and Different

In each row, circle the picture that is
the same as the first one.

Find the Match

Find and circle these things in the picture.

Birds and Insects

Draw lines from the birds to the word **bird**.
Draw lines from the insects to the word **insect**.

Cars and Trucks

Draw lines from the cars to the word **car**.
Draw lines from the trucks to the word **truck**.

Spot the Differences

Find and circle 6 differences between the two pictures.

Spot the Differences

Find and circle 6 differences between the two pictures.

Fruit and Vegetables

Circle the items that you might find in the fruit-and-vegetables section of a supermarket.

Clothes Shopping

Cross out the things that shouldn't
be in this clothing store.

Match the Opposites

Trace the lines to find the opposites.

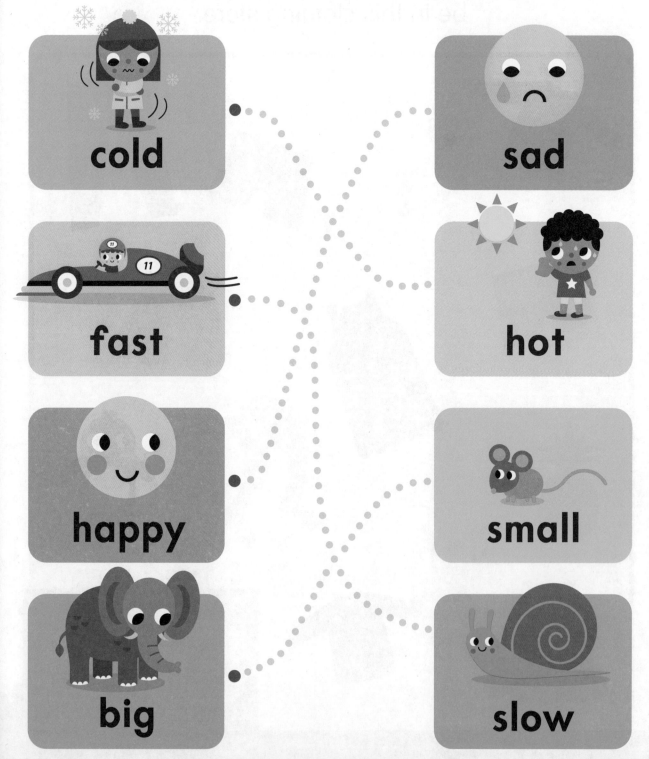

cold

sad

fast

hot

happy

small

big

slow

Find the Opposites

Draw lines to match the opposites.

wet

day

full

clean

night

dirty

dry

empty

Find the Opposites

Draw lines to match the opposites in the picture.

inside

up

outside

down

awake

high

asleep

Circle the Opposites

In each row, circle the opposite of the first word.

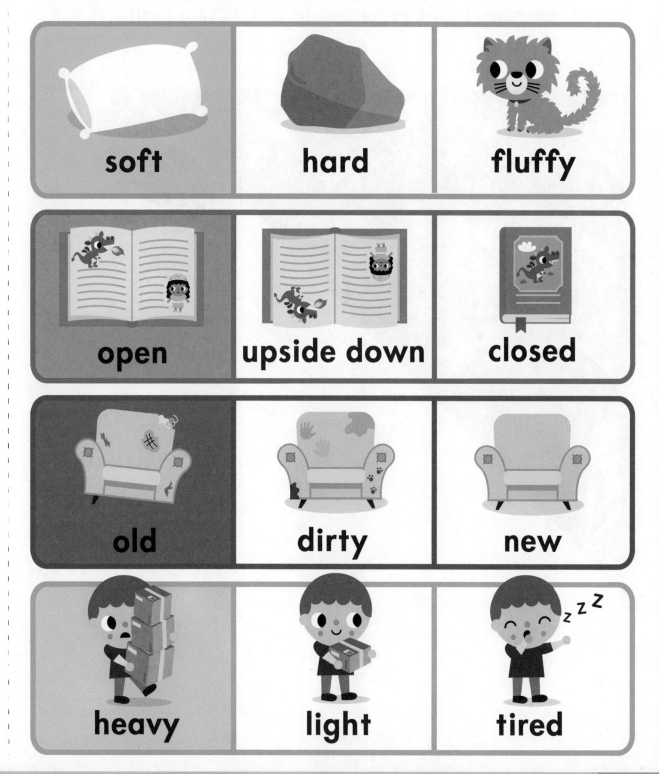

soft

hard

fluffy

open

upside down

closed

old

dirty

new

heavy

light

tired

Finish the Pattern

This pattern has 2 colors.
Use pencils or crayons to finish the pattern.

Finish the Pattern

This pattern has 3 colors.
Use pencils or crayons to finish the pattern.

What's Next?

These patterns repeat after every second image.
Circle the object that comes next in each pattern.

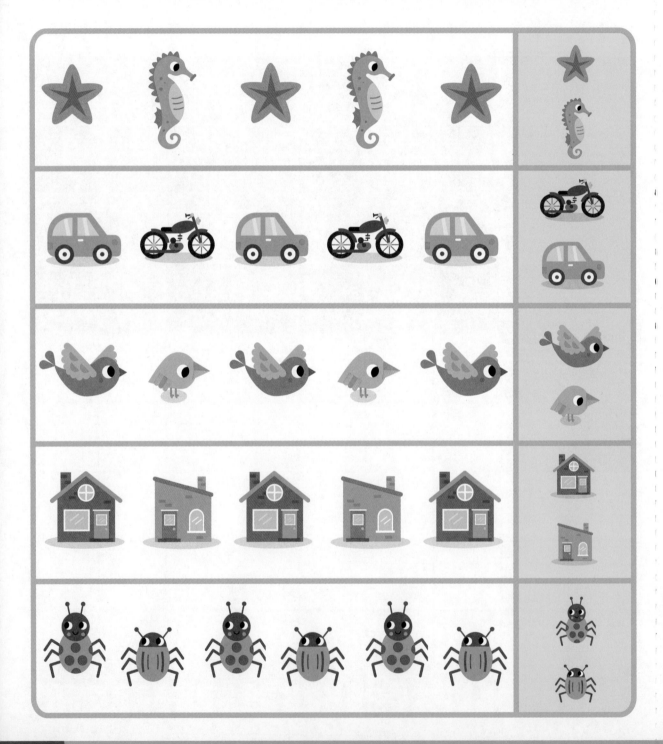

What's Next?

These patterns repeat after every third image.
Circle the object that comes next in each pattern.

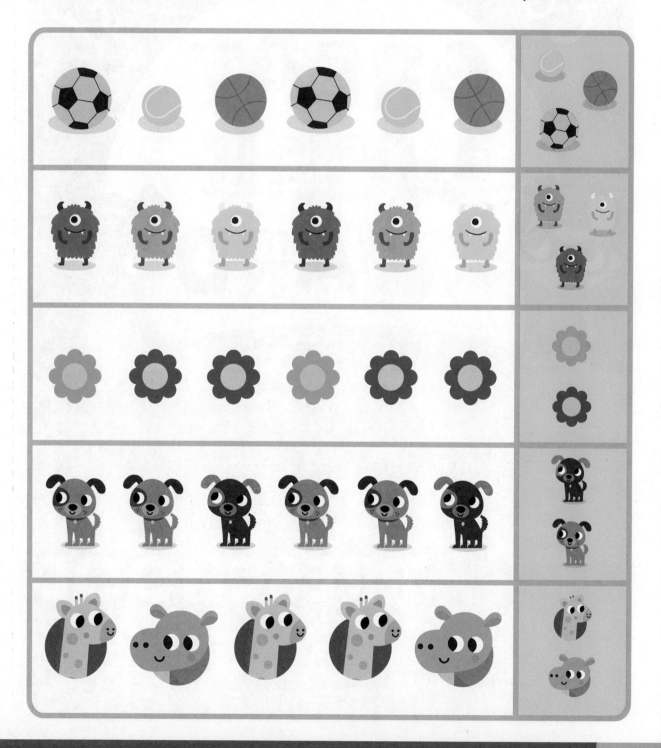

Congratulations!

GREAT WORK AWARD

Name: ....

has successfully completed

GIANT PRESCHOOL

Date: ....